LESSONS FROM
LEVITICUS

BIBLE STUDY AIDS *of William G. Heslop*

LESSONS

FROM

LEVITICUS

Inductive   Explanatory
Practical   Illustrative
Suggestive   Doctrinal
Typical

by

William G. Heslop, D.D., Litt. S.D.

KREGEL PUBLICATIONS
Grand Rapids, Michigan 49501

Lessons From Leviticus by W.G. Heslop.
Reprinted by Kregel Publications, a Division
of Kregel, Inc., under special arrangements
with the original publisher, Nazarene Pub-
lishing House. All rights reserved.

Library of Congress Catalog Card Number: 75-21895
ISBN 0-8254-2827-0

Kregel Publications edition 1975

Printed in the United States of America

CONTENTS

FOREWORD

I heard an educator say, "I consider an education is far more extensive if the student majored in History." It is none the less so when Religious History has been well included.

The Bible contains, not only the most ancient, but also the most reliable history. The book of Genesis deals with the beginnings and affords us the most reliable information concerning God's creation and His dealings with man in his primeval state.

The book of Exodus not only tells us of the deliverance of Israel from the relation of slaves and later organized into a nation, but connects us with Babylonian, Assyrian, and Egyptian history which reveals civilizations, literature, libraries, and laws well capable of directing a highly civilized commonwealth. The higher critics and evolutionists would have us believe that we relate to the "cave man," still lower to the "monkey family," and still farther back to the "cell" and "spectron," but the facts of history and archæology are proving that even as far back as Abraham, there was a civilization of surprising intelligence. It is folly for the higher critics to try to make us believe that the intelligence and literary ability of those days made it impossible for Moses to draft laws so capable of regulating the right conduct of a people, as that delivered to Israel!

The subject of this book—"Lessons from Leviticus"—deals with some of the most interesting study for any Bible student. At Sinai, God organized a nation—the nation of Israel—by which He proposed to judge the nations of the world from then until now and He has done it. He has not forgotten His promise to Abraham and the nation that mistreats the Jews has and will suffer for it. He declared that they were chosen to be a nation and people above all others (Deut. 7:6). Leviticus—the book of the law—contains a code peculiarly adapted to the Hebrews and their needs, thus sharply separating them from all other people, and elevating them to a higher and better standard than the nations about them. Its end and character are holiness. The tabernacle, the vessels, the offerings, the priest's garments, and all who approach Him whose name is holy, must themselves be holy. Leviticus, like the tabernacle, may appear rough and uninviting from the outside, but it is all glorious within. Those who with reverence will approach its portals, may first notice the rough "badger skins" without, but inside they will behold the glory of gold and "fine twined linen with blue, purple, and scarlet."

To the advantage and edification of the reader, I commend the author of this volume, Dr. Wm. G. Heslop. His publication of "Gems from Genesis," "Extras from Exodus," "Diamonds from Daniel," and "Riches from Revelation" and their wide circulation merit his sending forth this volume bearing its significant title and relation to the third book of the Pentateuch.

For many years Dr. Heslop has been a very special and close friend of mine and it gives me pleasure to recommend to the reading public, this rare volume of important Bible study. I predict an eager demand for this book among those who are desirous of valuable Bible knowledge.

Greensboro, N. C.   Winfred R. Cox

THEME OF THE BOOK

HOLINESS is the Grand Theme of the Book of Leviticus. A Holy God is seen providing a Holy Saviour who through the power of the Holy Spirit enables the Believer to worship God in the Beauty of Holiness.

Holiness is commanded, provided, obtained, enjoyed and maintained.

The Book of Leviticus insists on Holiness in Character, holiness in Conversation, holiness in Conduct, holiness in the heart, holiness in the life, holiness in the home, holiness in business, holiness in the house of God and holiness in worship.

Genesis is the Book of Beginnings.

Exodus is the Book of Redemption.

Leviticus is the Book of Worship.

"Begin with God" is the message of Genesis.

"Be Redeemed by the Blood of the Lamb" is the message of Exodus.

"Worship the Lord in the Beauty of Holiness" is the message of Leviticus.

THE AUTHENTICITY OF LEVITICUS

1. Inspiration is claimed by the Book itself.

"The Lord called unto Moses, and spake unto him." This is the opening sentence of the book and the closing sentence reads, "These are the commandments which the Lord commanded." These and similar expressions occur fifty-six times in the Book of Leviticus.

2. The veracity of Leviticus was unquestioned for more than twenty centuries.

So far as scholarship has been able to show the text of Leviticus is exactly the same today as it was when the sacred canon was established in the days of Ezra. Three thousand years have swept over this volume, and it stands today as steady and as immovable as Gibraltar.

3. Christ himself has declared in favor of its divine origin and dependability. Christ affirmed it to be the law of Moses (Luke 24:44).

The divine origin, authority and infallibility of Leviticus is settled by the signature and seal of Christ.

God's Book has safely passed through every storm which Satan has raised against it. The Bible is here to stay. God's Book like God's people is here to stay. Neither the Jew nor the Book written by the Jew can be destroyed. Fire has failed to burn it as water has failed to quench it. Edicts of kings, popes, and prelates have not been able to break its power. The more it is opposed the more it multiplies and grows. It is the Word of God which not only liveth but abideth forever. That Moses wrote the Pentateuch is plain to all who will follow their own feet.

1. "Moses was learned in all the wisdom of the Egyptians."

2. "Moses was mighty in words and deeds."

3. "The Lord said unto Moses, Write . . . in a book."

4. "Moses wrote all the words of the Lord."

5. "And Moses wrote this law."

6. "As I was with Moses so will I be with thee."

7. "God made known his ways unto Moses."

8. "The law was given by Moses."

9. "Moses truly said . . . a prophet shall the Lord your God raise up. . . ."

10. "Even to this day when Moses is read, the veil is upon their hearts."

11. "Offer the gift that Moses commanded."

12. "Moses, because of the hardness of your hearts, suffered you to put away your wives."

13. "For Moses said, Honour thy father and thy mother."

14. "As Moses lifted up the serpent in the wilderness even *so*."

15. "Had ye believed Moses ye would have believed me, for he wrote of me."

Were Matthew, Mark, Luke, John, Paul, Stephen, Joshua, David, and Christ all mistaken, ignorant, or lying?

Matthew 8:4
Matthew 19:8

Mark 7:10
John 3:14
John 5:45, 46

Acts 3:22
 2 Corinthians 3:15

Acts 7:22
Exodus 17:14

Exodus 24:3, 4
Psalm 102:7
John 1:17
Joshua 1:5

Deuteronomy 31:9

DIVISIONS

THE OFFERINGS

"The Bible of the Jews in our Lord's time was practically our Old Testament. For us its supreme sanction is that which it derived from Christ himself. . . . What was indispensable to the Redeemer must always be indispensable to the redeemed."—Professor G. A. Smith.

THE OFFERINGS

THE PROBLEM AND THE ANSWER

Lev. 1—7

The Problem:

How may a sinful man approach a holy God?

The Answer:

I. THE BURNT OFFERING

  1. A Bullock

     (1) A male

     (2) Without blemish

     (3) Slain

     (4) Blood shed

     (5) Blood sprinkled

     (6) Flayed

     (7) Cut into pieces

     (8) Body washed in water

     (9) Inwards washed in water

    (10) All burned with fire

This was a voluntary offering. The hand of the offerer was placed upon the head of the victim. The bullock was accepted for the sinner.

Christ is the only way of approach to God.

Christ is God's ox pulling us out of sin.

The Male speaks of the energy and manhood of the Master Puller, Christ.

Without Blemish sets forth Him of whom it was said, "I find no fault."

The Flaying sets forth the cruel beatings and smitings endured by our suffering substitute.

The Cutting reminds us of the seven bleeding wounds which he received on Calvary, and which he bore for our sakes.

The Washing speaks of inward and outward purity: Christ's holy walk and work.

The Burning typifies the consuming fire of God's wrath, which burned against Christ as the *Sin bearer*.

Thus and only thus is solved the problem of how a sinful man may approach a holy God.

    2. A lamb or goat
- (1) Male
- (2) Without blemish
- (3) Killed
- (4) Blood shed
- (5) Sprinkled
- (6) Cut in pieces
- (7) Inwards and legs washed
- (8) Burned with fire.

Christ was more than God's OX. He was also God's LAMB. Behold the OX of God, who will pull you out of your sin. Behold the LAMB of God, who beareth away all your sin.

3. Turtle doves or pigeons
    (1) Taken from their peaceful nest
    (2) Brought down to earth
    (3) To suffer and die.
        a. Head severed from body
        b. Crop torn out
        c. Feathers plucked
        d. Burned with fire

What shocking treatment. Why the ruthless tearing away of the crop and feathers of an innocent dove? Only thus could man be redeemed and brought nigh to God.

II. THE MEAL OFFERING
    1. Fine flour
    2. Oil
    3. Oil poured upon the flour
    4. Frankincense
    5. Burned upon the altar.

Christ is not only the OX of God and the LAMB of God; He is also the BREAD of God. Christ is not only the *PULLER* out of sin, sorrow, and the world, He is not only the suffering substitute, but He is also the *Bread* of life to man.

III. THE PEACE OFFERING
    1. A bullock
    2. Without blemish
    3. Slain
    4. Blood shed

5. Blood sprinkled
6. Hand of offerer laid upon head of offering
7. Burned with fire

Christ is not only our Bread, He is our *Peace*.

IV. THE SIN OFFERING
1. A Bullock
2. Young
3. Slain and burned
4. Without the Camp
5. Ashes carried and laid in a clean place.

Here provision was made for sins of ignorance, for sin is sin whether of omission or commission. Sins of ignorance must be atoned for as well as any and every other sin and Christ became our *sin* offering as well as our *peace* offering.

V. THE TRESPASS OFFERING
1. A Ram
2. Without blemish
3. Slain

The offerer must
  (1) Confess
  (2) Restore
  (3) Add one-fifth

What wondrous grace and condescending mercy is here manifested. Provision is made for every need of sinful man. The problem is solved; man, sinful man, may have access to a sinless God. "I am the way."

THE OVEN
THE PLATE
THE FRYING PAN

"Only melted gold is minted,
  Only moistened clay is moulded.
  Only softened wax receives the seal,
  Only broken, contrite hearts—
  Only these receive the mark,
  Of the Potter, as He turns us on His wheel
  Shaped and burned to take and keep the mould—
  The heavenly mark—the stamp of God's pure gold!"

2

THE OVEN
THE PLATE
THE FRYING PAN

Lev. 2:1-16

The Lord told Moses that "when any will offer a meat offering unto the Lord, his offering shall be of fine flour; and he shall pour oil upon it, and put frankincense thereon." If the offering was baked in *the oven* it was to be of unleavened cakes of fine flour mingled with oil or unleavened wafers anointed with oil. If the oblation was a meat offering baked in a pan or on a *flat plate,* it was to be of fine flour unleavened and mingled with oil. If the oblation was a meat offering baked in the *frying pan* it was to be of fine flour saturated with oil. The offering was an offering made by fire of a sweet savour unto the Lord. No meat offering was to be made with leaven, and no offering brought unto the Lord was to have any honey either in it or upon it.

These offerings beautifully typify our Lord Jesus Christ as the Bread of God. the Bread of angels, and the Bread of life to man. Fine flour is obtained by crushing, pounding, and beating. This sets forth the sufferings of our Lord Jesus Christ in His life and walk among men before He became the Bread of Life. The mingling with oil speaks of the Holy Spirit. There were three ways in which the flour was baked. The meat offering baked in *the oven* sets forth the sufferings of Christ which only the eye of God could see, for He gave His soul an offering for sin. The offering baked in a pan or *flat plate* sets forth the sufferings of Christ which all could see. The flat plate offering thus sets forth the public sufferings of Christ. The offering baked in the *frying pan* sets forth the sufferings of Christ which were partly seen and partly hidden from the gaze of man. The offering baked in the oven could not be seen by man at all. The offering baked in the frying pan was partly seen and partly hidden. The offering baked on the flat plate could be seen by man; thus these three offerings together set forth the sufferings of Christ, much of which only the eye of God saw and the heart of God felt and understood. The fine flour, even and smooth and saturated with oil, sets forth our Lord Jesus Christ as the Bread of Life. He was born of the Spirit, filled with the Spirit, and led of the Spirit—He was in truth saturated with the Holy Ghost.

The prohibition of honey and leaven is also very significant. Leaven is a type of the silent diffusive power of evil. Leaven is always a type of evil. Leaven is corruption; it causes inflation, produces puffing up and puffing out, and was never to be offered unto the Lord.

Honey is a type of natural, human sweetness. God cannot accept anything human, and not even our human niceties can merit the smile and approval of God.

Fine flour sets forth our Lord Jesus Christ as the true Bread that cometh down from heaven.

The frankincense sets forth His beautiful life which continually ascended to God.

The oil is an emblem of the Holy Spirit. The fine *flour* (Christ) with the *oil* (Holy Spirit) and the *frankincense* (Christ's holy life) was an offering unto the Lord. No leaven or evil, and no honey or mere human sweetness could be acceptable to God.

"Empires have perished away as a shadow, leaving behind them only their names; they have perished and their places know them no more, but *the Jews are still there,* standing apart from all other races, as in the days of Jesus Christ, one distinct and unique family in the midst of the confusion of all others; rich, though a thousand times despoiled; increasing in numbers and more united than ever, though scattered by a tempest of eighteen centuries to the extremities of the globe."

3

THE GOSPEL
ACCORDING TO MOSES

"It shall be accepted for him" (Lev. 1:4).

The Lord called unto Moses out of the tabernacle of the congregation and instructed him that if any man would bring an offering unto the Lord he must bring a male without blemish, and offer it of his own voluntary will at the door of the tabernacle of the congregation before the Lord. He must put his hand upon the head of the victim; then the victim would be accepted for him to make atonement for him. He was to kill the victim, cut it into his pieces, and burn it upon the altar. It was to be a burnt sacrifice, an offering made by fire of a sweet savour unto the Lord. The offering could be of the herd such as a bullock, or of the flocks such as a lamb or goat, or of the fowls such as turtle doves or young pigeons. Such offerings were to be the best, cleanest and finest that could possibly be obtained. They were to be without blemish and offered unto the Lord. If the offering was of the flocks such as a sheep or a goat the victim was to be cut into his pieces, the inwards and legs washed with water; and burned upon the altar. If the burnt sacrifice was of fowls such as turtle doves or young pigeons the head of the victim must be wrung off, and the blood wrung out at the side of the altar. The feathers of the harmless dove must be plucked away together with his crop and cast beside the altar. It was to be an offering made by fire of a sweet savour unto the Lord. These offerings typify our Lord Jesus Christ. The book of Leviticus is not a book which contains an obsolete economy, but is God's picture book of redemption. The book of Leviticus is not only a book applicable to our times, but is full of practical lessons and, like all other scripture, is profitable. The *Bullock* sets forth our Lord Jesus Christ as the true servant of God and the true servant of man. The bullock was to be killed. The flaying and cutting into pieces set forth the intense suffering of our Lord Jesus Christ. His body was broken, and His soul was made an offering for sin.

The bullock was to be a male without blemish and offered voluntarily. Christ was the strong Son of God, and was perfect, holy, and without blemish. When the offerer put his hand upon the head of the bullock and leaned heavily upon the bullock, in humble confession of sin, and identified himself with the victim, IT was accepted for him to make atonement for him.

In order to be accepted by God we must put our hand of faith upon Christ and thus leaning heavily upon Him, in humble confession, and identification, we shall be accepted in the beloved. Man is lost, guilty, depraved, and condemned; therefore he or an innocent victim must burn. Selah!

By identifying ourselves with Christ, He is accepted for us to make atonement for us. The cutting into His pieces, and ringing off the head, and plucking away the crop with the feathers, all set forth the suffering and agonies of our Lord Jesus Christ, who gave His back to the smiters and His face to those who plucked out the hair. The shocking treatment meted out to these innocent victims was a foreshadowing of the shocking treatment which would be meted out to the Lamb of God and our Gentle Dove of the heavens. The broken body, the disjointed bones, the flowing blood, the laying bare of the flesh, the burning flames, the binding of the innocent victims, the leading of them to a place of slaughter, the knife and fire together with the mangled flesh of the harmless victims, set forth the awful sufferings and agonies of the crucified Christ. His blood was shed; His flesh was laid bare; His body was broken, His bones were disjointed; His face was marred more than any man's; He was bound to the altar and led to the slaughter; yet He opened not His mouth. He was the Lamb of God and the gentle Dove of the heavens. The necessity of these offerings shows us the exceeding sinfulness of sin. The meek and innocent dove was brought from its peaceful home in the heavens to suffer and die. The harmless, winsome, affectionate Dove of the heavens was brought down to earth to have its flesh mangled, the feathers plucked from its body, its crop torn away, its head pinched off its shoulders, and its life taken in a violent death upon the altar. Upon the wood that is upon the fire, it became a sweet savour offering unto the Lord. What striking pictures! And all setting forth the exceeding sinfulness of sin and the awful sufferings and sacrifice of Christ to make an atonement for us! God's sanctuary in the Old Testament had the appearance of a solemn slaughter house. Sacrifice and shedding of blood was the basis of acceptable worship in the Old Testament, for without shedding of blood there is no remission of sins.

THE PRIEST

This is the Book of Worship, Sacrifice, and Priesthood. Exodus closes with God's Tabernacle in the midst of the tents of Israel. Leviticus opens with the Law of offerings. *In order for the Holy One to dwell among sinners, and accept their service, there must be atonement by sacrifice and mediation by priesthood. The elect tribe, Levi, of the elect nation, represent the Appointed Day's-Man between God and men.*

Dr. A. T. Pierson

4

THE PRIEST

Lev. 8—9

Let us here notice in detail the different garments worn by the High Priest.

1. The Breastplate
2. The Ephod
3. The Robe
4. The Broidered Coat
5. The Mitre
6. The Girdle
7. Linen Breeches

1. The Breastplate.

This typifies the tender love of the Lord Jesus Christ as the Great High Priest of our profession.

2. The Ephod

The gold sets forth Christ's deity, the blue typifies a heavenly Christ, the purple speaks of a kingly Christ, the scarlet foreshadows a suffering Christ, the fine linen sets forth His spotless life here on earth, and the cunning work typifies the work of the Holy Spirit. The curious girdle of the Ephod was a striking symbol of the SERVANT, who took a towel and girded himself. The breastplate indicates affection, the shoulder speaks of *power* to carry, and the Urim and Thummim indicate *wisdom*. Here are wisdom, love, and power united in one.

3. The Robe of the Ephod

This robe was all of *blue* thus setting forth the *heavenly* Christ. Our High Priest with the words "Holiness unto the Lord" entered the presence of God having obtained eternal redemption for us. All these things have a *voice* for us today. The tinkling bell (testimony), witnessing to the people that their Priest was alive, together with pomegranates (fruitfulness), teach us that our lip confession must be supported by a life of fruitfulness, a life that shows that we walk even as He walked.

The SHOULDER is the place of strength, strength to carry.

The BREAST or BOSOM speaks of rest and comfort.

The HEART speaks of affection and love.

The HANDS and ARMS stand for safety and support.

The FOREHEAD stands for remembrance.

The WINGS stand for protection and power.

The GOLDEN BELL speaks of testimony, DIVINE testimony.

The POMEGRANATE speaks of fruitfulness.

It is interesting to remember here the difference between the food of Egypt mentioned in the Bible and the food of Canaan.

Leeks and onions grow in the ground. We must stoop and bend to obtain them. Grapes, pomegranates, and figs grow up in the heavens. We must straighten up and stretch out or else we shall never get them. Grapes, figs, and pomegranates also are full of seeds. Seeds speak to us of future fruitfulness and life.

The *linen breeches* speak of the holy walk and devoted life of Christ.

The *girdle* speaks of service.

The *mitre* speaks of the crown and reminds us again that Christ is not only a Savior and Sanctifier but also a Prince and coming King.

The quality of THE FLOUR in the offering bespeaks the intrinsic worthiness of the character of Christ.

"Holy, harmless, undefiled . . . "

The OIL witnesses to the fact that Christ's birth, words and works were the result of the anointing of the Holy Spirit.

The FRANKINCENSE which produced a pleasing odour tells of the delectability, attractiveness, invitingness, fascination and charm of Christ.

Fine flour, oil and frankincense are things most holy unto the Lord. They set forth the graces, faultlessness, and exquisite virtues of the spotless Son of God.

The BRUISED corn suggests the sufferings of Christ for "it pleased the Lord to bruise him."

Reproach had broken His heart. A crushed, bruised and suffering Savior is man's only hope.

"By his stripes we are healed."

The presence of Salt signifies that His heart, life and lips were full of grace.

The absence of HONEY reveals the fact that the sweetness, and attractiveness of Christ were not mere human sweetness, courtesy and culture.

The absence of LEAVEN witnesses to the truth that, in Christ there was no evil, no corrupting tendencies, and no fault.

THE SANCTIFICATION
OF THE PRIESTS

"Just as the scarlet line is found everywhere in the cordage of the British Navy, cut it where you will, Christ is found everywhere in the Old Testament."

THE SANCTIFICATION
OF THE PRIESTS

"This is the thing which the Lord commanded" (8:5).

I. AARON
1. Of a special tribe.
2. Free from bodily sickness.
3. Devoted to sacred work.
4. Did not engage in temporal affairs after his anointing.
5. Washed in water.
6. Anointed with oil.
7. Specially clothed.
8. Suitably crowned.
9. Made an atonement for all the people.
10. Interceded for the transgressors.
11. Entered into the presence of God.
12. Judged the people.
13. Decided all matters of controversy.
14. Came out from the presence of God.
15. Blessed the people.
16. God's will was his supreme delight.

Aaron was not only to be physically sound but he must be properly mated by choosing a pure virgin for his bride. His children also must be holy. How significant all this becomes when viewed in the light of our High Priest, even our Lord Jesus Christ.

Christ was free from bodily sickness and infirmity, devoted to sacred work, washed and anointed; and having made atonement for all the people and having entered into the presence of God for us, He shall come again to bless His people, the Bridegroom will take unto Himself His bride (a pure virgin). He *was* the Prophet like unto Moses. He *is* the Priest like unto Aaron and Melchizedek. He *shall be* the King of kings and Lord of Lords.

II. AARON'S SONS
1. Sons by birth.
2. Separated.
3. Holy.
4. Perfect.
5. Peculiar.
6. Devoted to the worship and service of God.
7. Washed in water.
8. Anointed (1) with blood
              (2) with oil.
9. Clothed.
10. Offered sacrifices to God.
11. Interceded for the brethren.
12. Instructed the people.
13. Enjoyed direct access to God.
14. Kept the holy fires burning.
15. Helped in the erection of the tabernacle.
16. God made special provision for their every need.
17. Blessed the people in the name of the Lord.
18. Were abandoned to God and the service of God.

The sons of Aaron typify believers as Aaron typified Christ, the Great High Priest. Believers are *sons by birth*. We do not obtain admittance into the family of God by signing a card or joining the church. God's sons and priests are a separated people; they are peculiar in ways, speech, dress, habits of life, employment, and enjoyments. Blood has been applied and they are anointed by the sevenfold Spirit. By offering the sacrifices of righteousness they are enabled to make intercession for the saints. God's sons and ministers enjoy access to God and keep the fires of holy love and zeal burning on the altar of their hearts. All are co-workers with God in the building of the spiritual tabernacle, for which the materials are being blasted out of the quarry of sin by the gospel of the grace of God!

Oh, for more sons and servants abandoned to the will of God and the service of man. Such were the sons of Aaron and such are the sons and ministers of Jesus Christ.

THE ANOINTING OIL
and
THE ANOINTING

"At Aaron's consecration the precious ointment was not only poured upon his head, but ran down in rich profusion upon his body and upon his priestly garments (Psalm 133:2). And now we behold our Aaron, our great High Priest, who has passed through the heavens, Jesus the Son of God, standing in the holiest in heaven. 'Thou didst love righteousness and didst hate iniquity,' is the divine encomium passed upon Him, 'therefore God, thy God, anointed thee with the oil of gladness above thy fellows.' He, the anointed, stands above and for His anointed brethren, and from Him, the Head, the unction of the Holy Ghost descended on the *Day of Pentecost. It was poured in rich profusion upon His mystical body.* It has been flowing down ever since, and will continue to do so until the last member shall have been incorporated with Himself, and so anointed by the one Spirit into the one body, which is the Church."— A. J. GORDON, D.D.

6

THE ANOINTING OIL

Moses was commanded to take principal spices: pure myrrh, sweet cinnamon, sweet calamus, and cassia, together with oil of olives and make an oil of holy ointment, an holy anointing oil.

MYRRH eases pain and extracts soreness. This points to the death of Christ.

Cinnamon is hot spice. As a result of Christ's death it is our unspeakable privilege and responsibility to be baptized with the Holy Ghost and fire and keep hot. The lukewarm shall be spewed out.

Calamus speaks of sweetness. Holiness and sweetness go together. Sour holiness is a contradiction in terms and yet there seems a plentiful supply. Unkind holiness, unmerciful holiness, uncharitable holiness, vinegar holiness, clabber holiness, sour holiness, seem impossibilities, but unfortunately we have them all with us as certain as we have the poor always with us.

Cassia is a soothing spice. Oh, how holiness soothes! Christ can soothe away the anxious cares and fears. He can touch the fevered brow and soothe the troubled heart.

The Olive Oil is the last thing mentioned. Oil is a type of the Holy Spirit. Oil feeds, lubricates, keeps things running smoothly, and causes the face to shine. A plentiful supply of oil will stop wear and tear and breakdown. All this speaks of the anointing Christ. Oh, for His anointing to abide in us and on us.

This holy anointing oil was not put upon strangers, for it is not for sinners or the world, neither was it to be put on the flesh or carnality, nor was it to be imitated or copied.

The Holy Ghost does not come upon sinners or backsliders. Christ does not anoint carnality. He kills carnality first and then anoints. Holiness is not for the world—the holy anointing oil was to be put upon consecrated people for service. The baptism with the Holy Spirit is for consecrated people; the fulness of the blessing is for cleansing and power for service. The blessing is not for feasting and entertainment, noise or show, but for work, labor, service, and soul winning; NOT to stretch us on the floor, knock out chair bottoms, smash church seats, dance the dust out of carpets, roll in straw, yell like an Indian or be still like a corpse. The baptism with the Holy Ghost and fire is for purity and power for service. It is that we might be witnesses and saviors of OTHERS.

THE ANOINTING

I. The Word ANOINT Has Several Meanings

1. To consecrate

   The first mention of the word anointed is in Genesis 31:13 where Jacob anointed the pillar at Bethel. In this passage the word means to consecrate, sanctify, set apart.

2. To pour out
   Here is set forth the pentecostal experience of
   (1) Cleansing
   (2) Filling
   (3) Power

3. To rub in and rub on
   Here is set forth the idea of lubrication after we
   obtain the cleansing and fulness.

4. To fatten
   A thin, gaunt, skinny body is bad enough but
   what must a skinny soul look like?

II. PERSONS WHO RECEIVED THE ANOINTING:

1. Prophets
   Anointing is necessary if we are to faithfully
   declare the will and word of God.

2. Priests
   Anointing is necessary if we are to pray and
   prevail with God.

3. Kings
   Anointing is necessary if we are to govern either
   ourselves or others.
   To be men of power we must be anointed.
   To be men of authority we must be anointed.

III. THE ANOINTING WAS APPLIED TO:

1. The Head
   We need the anointing for wisdom, guidance,
   direction, teaching.

2. The Face
   The anointing is necessary in order to shine for
   God and adorn the doctrine of Christ.

3. The Feet
   We must be anointed if we are to walk as He
   walked: well pleasing in the sight of God.

4. The Eyes
   To see as He saw and to enjoy the vision of
   glory as John, or of God as Isaiah, we must be
   anointed with the Holy Ghost. "When he saw
   the multitudes he was moved."
   When we are anointed and see as he saw we
   too shall be moved.

IV. THE ANOINTING WAS USED FOR:

1. Refreshing
   If we are to keep fresh, alert, alive, and active
   we must be anointed.

2. Purifying
   If Esther needed anointing before she appeared
   before an earthly king how much more do we
   need the anointing to appear before the King
   of kings.

3. Preparing weapons for war
   "Arise, ye princes, anoint the shield," said
   Isaiah. While the weapons of our warfare are
   not carnal but spiritual, we, nevertheless, need
   to have our weapons anointed.

4. Preserving

"The Lord saveth his anointed," said David and in full sympathy with these words as well as in complete harmony with them are the words of Paul: "The very God of peace sanctify you wholly and . . . preserve you blameless."

5. Protecting

"Touch not mine anointed," says the Holy Spirit.

If it was necessary that Christ, the Son of God, should be anointed before beginning His work how much more is it necessary in our case.

If Christ, who was born of the Spirit and filled with the Spirit and led by the Spirit, must needs be anointed by the Spirit how dare we attempt a work for God without the anointing.

THE SIN
OF
NADAB AND ABIHU

"Sin is but a *bitter-sweet* at best; and the fine colors of the serpent do by no means make amends for the smart and poison of the sting."—South.

"He that hath tasted the bitterness of sin will fear to commit it; and he that hath felt the sweetness of mercy will fear to offend it."—Charnock.

"Men first wound their consciences and then sear them by repeated acts of sin; and you know that ice which is at first so tremulous and feeble, that it will not bear a pebble, yet by a few days' freezing will bear a cart. So it is with the sinner."—Bates.

"Every sin is an imitation of the devil, and creates a kind of hell in the heart."—Hervey.

"No sin can be little, because there is no little God to sin against."—Brooks.

7

THE SIN
OF
NADAB AND ABIHU

Lev. 10

Nadab and Abihu were the two sons of Aaron. Each took his censer and put fire therein, put incense thereon, and offered strange fire before the Lord. Suddenly, there went out fire from the Lord and devoured them, and they died before the Lord.

Aaron held his peace, and the two young men were carried outside of the camp and buried. Aaron and his other sons were forbidden to mourn over them. In order to understand the untimely death of Nadab and Abihu it is necessary to understand something about the priesthood with its duties and privileges. All people have had their priests. Job was his own priest as also was Adam before him. Abel and Noah offered sacrifices to God. Jethro, Moses' father-in-law, was a priest of Midian. Aaron was the priest of the children of Israel. He was taken, with his sons, anointed, clothed, and crowned as the high priest of Jehovah. The first seven chapters of Leviticus set forth the sacrifices necessary to atone for sin. The eighth and ninth chapters of Leviticus set forth the office of the priesthood. The sinner needs a sacrifice, whereas the believer needs a priest. Christ is both the sacrifice and the priest. The lamb, bullock, ram, dove, goat, and pigeon set forth Christ as the sacrifice for the sin of the world. Aaron speaks of Christ as our High Priest now in the presence of God for us. Sin separated man from God. There is a chasm between man and God and a mediator is necessary. In the case of Israel, Moses and Aaron were their mediators. At stated times they were to appear in the presence of God in the Holy of Holies and offer incense unto the Lord and make atonement for the children of Israel. This was the thing which the Lord commanded to be done. Moses and Aaron were divinely called, washed with pure water, clothed, and girded for service. They were consecrated for their holy office, and, with blood appeared before the presence of God. Aaron with his hands dripping with blood, lifted them up and out towards the people and blessed them. The special privilege of Aaron was to enter the holy of holies and thus make an atonement for the children of Israel.

We need to be reminded that any kind of fire will not please the Lord and that any kind of worship will not satisfy the Lord. Some of our conceptions of anything . . . anyway . . . anywhere . . . anyhow, in connection with our worship and service, is not pleasing to the Lord. Nadab and Abihu took their own way, ignored the Word of the Lord, and perished in their iniquity. Yesterday, the people were shouting. Today they are sighing. Yesterday they were obedient and happy (Lev. 9:23, 24). Today they are disobedient and wailing. Life is full of such tremendous contrasts. Disobedience means distress, disturbance and death.

Aaron held his peace. The honor and glory of God were more to him than his own sons. Looking through heaven's glasses, knowing that death ended the earthly relationship, and recognizing that his sons had wilfully ignored the word of the Lord, he bowed his head to the divine verdict, and without mourning or uncovering his head or rending his clothes, without even attending their funeral, Aaron permitted his sons to be buried. Every first, wilful, and serious offence against God and His Word has met with instant judgment at the hands of God as a warning to all others that ultimate punishment is sure. Israel perished in the wilderness as a warning to all holiness rejecters that they too shall perish (1 Thess. 4:7, 8). Achan was stoned to death and his body covered with a heap of stones as a warning to all transgressors that their sin will find them out. Nadab and Abihu were suddenly smitten by God as a warning to us that all wilful ignoring of the Word of the Lord and going our own way, will end in death. Korah, Dathan, and Abiram went alive to hell. Rebellion against God and slandering of God's people, will land us in hell.

Ananias and his wife Sapphira, having kept back part of the price, with a false profession on their lips, and a lie in their hearts dropped dead in their tracks as a warning to all that the wages of sin is death. The God of the Bible is not a wishy-washy, dilly-dally wax doll. All men shall discover that "the wages of sin is death," "the soul that sinneth it shall die," and that it is a fearful thing to fall into the hands of the living God. Better consider *the end* of sin before beginning in a life of sin. Think a moment on the two sons of Aaron.

Yesterday! the shouts of praise. Today! death and destruction. Yesterday! the wedding march. Today! the funeral dirge. Life is full of such tragic and cruel contrasts. Births and deaths. The cradle and then the coffin. Bridals and burials. Weddings and funerals. Gladness and gloom. Mirth and mourning.

Nadab and Abihu were sons. They had been born right. They had been called, cleansed and commissioned. Becoming disobedient, rebellious, wilful, stiff-necked and then taking matters into their own hands and acting according to their own will, wisdom and ways they were smitten and slain. They died in the sanctuary. Died while performing service. Died in the meeting house.

Each first offense against the revealed and known Word of God meets with instant punishment as a warning to all of that ultimate vengeance which is certain to overtake all violators of the law of God. Achan, Korah, Nadab, Ananias, et al, warns us as to the inevitable consequences which follow disobedience.

The solemn and striking silence of Aaron proves that the judgment meted out to his two sons was a righteous and deserving judgment, "Aaron held his peace."

Others less spiritual may prate against the righteous ways of God but "Aaron held his peace." He knew his sons and he knew God, "Aaron held his peace." His two sons were dead, but, "Aaron held his peace." The father knew the wickedness and the waywardness of his two sons and the cause of God meant more to Aaron than the life of his sons and hence "Aaron held his peace."

The honor and glory of God was more to Aaron than the well being of his sinful sons. He loved God more than he loved his family. His love for his children did not blind him to the claims of God and so "Aaron held his peace." Faith and trust never grumbles and never complains. Aaron looked at things with and through heaven's glasses, wearing holiness goggles he was protected and safeguarded from selfish conclusions.

Human selfishness makes cynics and skeptics. Faith holds its peace. Aaron realized that all earthly bonds were broken by death. He knew that all earthly relationships were severed and ended by death and hence he "held his peace."

If loved ones are lost they will be lost despite the love of God, the sufferings of Christ, the entreaties of the Holy Spirit, the warnings of conscience, the exhortations of ministers, and the prayers and cries of sanctified saints.

He that loveth Father or Mother, son or daughter more than Christ is not worthy of Him.

Neither mourning nor weeping was permitted at the funeral. Not a tear was shed. God's government and glory were more important than the interests of two giddy and rebellious sons.

Selfish sorrow was forbidden. Wholesome lessons were learned by all. The believer knows that all God's ways are right and best, that He is too wise to err and too good to be unkind.

Nadab and Abihu rejected the Word of God and were ruined world without end.

Despising God's Word and will and ways Nadab was damned. Offering strange and unholy fire kindled the wrath of God against them and they perished in the house of prayer.

CLEAN AND UNCLEAN

"Observe the meadow-lark. He lifts his head in the sunshine and tells in liquid melody his joy in the light, the air, the meadow-grass and flowers. When it rains, he finds the best shelter he can and awaits uncomplainingly the return of warmth and brightness.

I wish there were more people like him.

Observe the mole. He burrows along beneath the ground. If, by any chance, a ray of light penetrates to him, he quickly digs deeper to avoid it. His days are dark and he likes them that way. The more profound his gloom the better he is satisfied. The thought of singing never enters his head. All his time is taken up with burrowing. He has none left for rejoicing.

I wish there were fewer people like him."

8

CLEAN AND UNCLEAN

Lev. 10—13

There is a tremendous difference between a sheep and a pig. If a lamb falls into a mud puddle it will bleat until it is taken out while the hog will hunt for the dirt ditch, wallow in it and enjoy it. Animals that chew the cud and part the hoof were pronounced clean. Christians must not only eat right but also walk right. We ought to diligently meditate on the Word of God (chew the cud) and then walk uprightly (part the hoof).

An animal chewing the cud but dividing not the hoof was unclean. Both the food and the walk must be right. The Word and the Walk must be holy.

Animals like the wily burrowing coney were all unclean to the Israelites. *Nosing* around makes all unclean. Pushing the nose into other people's property and possessions constituted uncleanness in the people.

The coney is always covering, and hiding things, reminding us that he that covereth his sins shall not prosper.

Fish with fins and scales were clean, teaching us the necessity of developing good fins with which we may make good progress and also good scales by which we may keep out the elements as we progress. It is possible to live in a godless home, work in an unholy atmosphere and yet keep clean and pure.

We are IN the world but not OF the world. FINS in order to move forward and make progress, and scales in order to keep free from contamination and defilement.

Like the lily in the mud pond we may be kept sweet and clean.

Birds with wings and yet spending most of the time walking and hopping around on the ground were also declared unclean to the children of Israel.

Wings are intended for the heavens and we are expected to mount up with wings. Our citizenship is in heaven and we may not spend all our time picking up corn and crumbs. "Oh! how we grovel here below." Fowl feeding on flesh were also prohibited. Believers are not to be buzzards and vultures but like sheep.

The brute creation also has its instruction and lessons for the beloved of God.

Living by mere impulse, following no law, but the law of its own selfish animal desires and pleasures, unable to walk uprightly, always bent earthward, without conscience and destined to perish, the brute creation passes on without God, without prayer, and without hope. The filthiness and sensuality of the hog, the stupid stubbornness of the ass, the balkiness of the mule, the fierceness and terror of the tiger, the sluggishness of the sloth, the pride of the peacock, the crooked and crawling and lousy lizards, the venomous reptiles all have lessons for those who love God and long for that holiness without which no man shall see the Lord.

The history of the world is largely a history of wars, strife, persecution, jealousy, envy, hatred, malice, murder, bloodshed and butchery. The heart of man by nature is a cage of unclean birds and a den of fierce wild and untamable beasts.

Behold the burning jealousies in the breast of womankind and the murder in the minds of men.

Look at the hatreds, and hell and lust in the soul of sinners. Oh, the spitefulness, rape, wickedness, lawlessness and diabolism in the unsanctified hearts of humans.

Think of the poor unfortunate sons of men awaiting the gallows, the electric chair, and the lethal chambers.

Oh, the beastliness and the bestiality of man. Carnality in saint or sinner is the beginning of hell. It is Satan's spark of damnation in the soul. We must get rid of it or be damned.

FINS AND SCALES

"To many the Old Testament is little more than a collection of eastern stories, because they have not seen Christ in it. Once Christ is seen every line of it becomes radiant with meaning. You may have seen a card with a picture of some rural scene, and underneath the words, '*Find* out *the face*.' You hold the card this way and that way until all of a sudden you behold a face. When once you have found that, you can never look at the card again without seeing it. You only wonder you did not see it before."

9

FINS AND SCALES

The Lord commanded Moses and Aaron to inform the children of Israel that they were not only a peculiar people, with peculiar laws, peculiar ways, and a peculiar worship, but that their diet also was to be peculiar. In accordance with this, instructions were given as to what kind of beasts may, and may not, be eaten. Animals that parted the hoof, and were cloven footed, and chewed the cud were permitted as food. Animals, such as the camel, because he chewed the cud but did not divide the hoof were unclean unto the children of Israel. The coney, the hare, and the swine were pronounced unclean and their flesh was not to be eaten.

Fish with *fins and scales* were permitted to be eaten but fish without fins and scales were to be an abomination unto them.

Fowls that creep, going upon all four, were also to be an abomination unto the children of Israel. Animals that went upon all four paws among all the beasts were all unclean unto the Israelites.

All these things have a meaning for us in this present dispensation. All Scripture is given by inspiration of God and is profitable. There was a reason for Herod being called a fox, the Gentiles, dogs, the false professors, goats, and holiness fighters, vipers. There is a profound difference between a hog and a sheep as may be seen when they fall into the mud. The hog enjoys it, wallows in it, and does not want to come out of it. The sheep hates the dirt. It bleats piteously until it is pulled out of the mud puddle.

The character of our outward walk, and the nature of our digesting that which we eat, have much to do with our being unclean or clean. The cow diligently gathers up the pasture and calmly lies down to assimilate that which has been gathered. "Blessed is the man that walketh not [the hoof] . . . but . . . in his law doth he meditate [chewing the cud]." The inward life and the outward walk must go together. Some people eat all right spiritually, but after they leave the meeting house they do not walk right. We must eat right and walk right if we are to be pronounced clean by our great high Priest. The ugliness and the spitefulness of the camel, the burrowing secretive ways of the coney, together with the filthiness and sensuality of the hog, are all pictures of the ways of sin. The stupid stubbornness of the ass, the sluggishness of the sloth, the ferocity and bloodthirstiness of the tiger, together with the strutting, proud peacock, have lessons for us today. Vultures, buzzards, lizards, and the poisonous, loathsome, hateful, dangerous snake and viper, each has its lesson for us today. The raven with its beak and claws has a message for all lovers of the Bible. The sight of any of these creatures would remind a Jew of his own sin and of the holiness of God.

FINS enable the fish to move through the water; SCALES keep it dry while it is moving through the water. The fins enable the fish to force his way through the element in which it breathes, lives, moves and has its being, and to pass rapidly on to another place while the scales keep out the elements as it is progressing through the water. Spiritual fins enable us to move in and through the world, and spiritual scales testify that we are not of the world. Our fins enable us to make progress, while our scales keep out the defiling element around us. We are IN the world but we are not OF the world. We need good spiritual fins and scales.

BIRDS with wings, which were made for the heavens, were unclean if they spent most of their time on the earth, crawling, creeping, and groveling on the ground. Those birds which fed on flesh, and those which could eat anything, and those which had the power to soar into the heavens but groveled on the earth, were all unclean.

As children of God we are made for the heavens and only stay on the earth sufficiently long enough to pick up a grain of wheat (food), and then fly back into the heavenly places where we belong. All these things have a spiritual meaning for us today.

Whether we eat or drink or whatsoever we do, do all for the glory of God.

These truths are emphasized again and again in the book of Leviticus.

THE GOSPEL
OF
THE TWO BIRDS

"Christ crucified and risen, is the one center of all the ways and purposes of God. The Cross of Calvary is no mere incident in the world's history; it is the great event to which all the past looked forward, and all the future will look back. The Cross is the manifestation of God's love; it is the proof of God's justice; it is the foundation of all His purposes; and it is the channel for the outflow of His grace to a perishing world. Christ is the great subject of the Scriptures. Give the Lord Jesus His true place, and all is clear both in the Bible and history. Ignore Christ and the Bible is a puzzle, and the world an enigma. Confessedly "Great is the mystery" of the incarnation; but, once accepted, it is the key to every other mystery."

10

THE TWO BIRDS

Lev. 14

In the case of a leper who sought cleansing from his leprosy it was necessary, first of all, that the leper be brought unto the priest. The priest was to go forth out of the camp and two birds, alive and clean, together with cedar wood, scarlet, and hyssop were provided. One of the birds was to be killed in an earthen vessel over running water. The living bird was then to be taken and dipped in the blood of the bird that had been killed, then was let loose into the open field. As the bird went up into the heavens, atoning blood was sprinkled on those beneath. The leper was to wash his clothes and shave off all his hair and wash himself in water. After that, he was permitted to come into the camp. After seven days he was to shave all his beard, his eyebrows, and his head. Having washed his clothes and his flesh in water, he was pronounced clean.

Leprosy is a perfect type of sin. Leprosy is an internal blood disease. In its infant stages it is not easily detected, is gradual in its development, and is one of the most loathsome and offensive of maladies. It separates from friends and loved ones and cannot be cured by any earthly, human means. Life and comeliness are gradually

eaten away by the dreadful disease until finally, it is
necessary for the leper to go to the abode of the lepers,
where, becoming more and more insensible to his real
condition, he passes from time to eternity. Leprosy
ends in death and it is a great Bible picture of inbred
sin. God set His people on the lookout for it, and when
discovered, it was immediately made known to the priest,
and everything affected had to be dealt with and washed
in pure water or burned with fire. Inbred sin in the soul
of man is a dreadful malady. The great disease of the
human race is INTERNAL for which there is no human
cure. Carnality is an internal malady which gradually
works out and eats away all spiritual life and comeliness.
Unless we get rid of it before we die it will separate us
from all the holy. To the eternal abode of spiritual
lepers we must go. When carnality is first discovered
we should immediately make it known to our great High
Priest, and by the washing of regeneration followed by
the burning of pentecostal fire we shall be purified and
receive the witness that we are clean.

The dead bird sets forth Christ dying for us, the just
for the unjust and the innocent for the guilty. The living
bird sets forth Christ who rose again for our justifica-
tion. The dead bird speaks of Christ delivered up for
our trespasses, while the living bird speaks of Christ
rising again and ascending on high where He ever liveth
to make intercession for us. The gentle birds of the
heavens were taken from their peaceful home and brought
down to earth to suffer and die. They were mangled,

crushed, and killed for the sins of others. Christ, the meek, gentle, and innocent dove of the heavens, was brought down to earth. He suffered and bled and died and having risen again, ascended on high to intercede for us.

Everything of nature, such as hair, and beard, and eyebrows, and all nature's adornments were to be cut off. Everything that was grown as a result of age and experience the leper must shave off. He must be prepared to be a very peculiar person and die out to all the niceties of nature.

God's people have ever been a peculiar people, with peculiar ways, and peculiar laws. We must be willing to be different from all other people on the face of the earth. Being pronounced clean by our great High Priest speaks of the witness of the Spirit. The leper cleansed by atoning blood and anointed by holy oil was pronounced clean. The jealous care of Jehovah over the habits and practices of His people Israel plainly declares that without holiness no man shall see the Lord.

THE DAY OF ATONEMENT

The Old Testament is more than a collection of historical tales. It was not written to give us either the origin of sin, or Satan, or the origin of the Jewish people. It is more than a book illustrating Oriental manners and customs. It was not written to supply Sunday stories for children.

The Old Testament is God's picture book of New Testament truths necessary for salvation here and heaven hereafter.

> "The New is in the Old contained
> The Old is by the New explained."

The Old Testament is the alabaster box of precious ointment. The New Testament reveals the fragrance when broken.

11

THE DAY OF ATONEMENT

The Scapegoat

Lev. 16:1-34

The day of atonement was the greatest event of the year for the children of Israel. Aaron, with the linen mitre upon his head and clothed with the holy linen coat and linen breeches, and girded with a linen girdle, was commanded to take of the congregation of Israel two kids of the goats. The two goats were to be taken and presented before the Lord. One of these goats was called the scapegoat.

The scapegoat was led into the wilderness, bearing upon its head and in its body all the sins of the people. The other goat was killed, and Aaron took the blood within the vail and sprinkled the mercy seat; and thus made an atonement for all the sins of all Israel. The countless, unnoticed, unrecognized, and unconfessed sins of all the people, with all their transgressions and defilements, were atoned for on this all important day, called the great day of atonement.

One of the goats having died, the living goat, called the scapegoat, carried away all the sins (confessed and unconfessed, noticed and unnoticed, forgiven and unforgiven sins), of all the people into a land of separation and forgetfulness.

The two goats received upon their heads the sin of the people. Then, one of them was led to the slaughter and died, the innocent dying for the guilty. Then the living goat was led forth by a fit man into the wilderness, bearing away all the iniquities of the people unto a land not inhabited, to pass out of sight and never to be seen again any more forever.

It seems strange, at first, that Christ should be typified by a goat. We can understand Christ being likened unto a lamb, a dove, a ram, a bullock, and a red heifer, but for Him to be typified by a goat seems strange. The *lamb* speaks of Christ as the meek, lowly, and submissive, unmurmuring suffering One. The *dove* speaks of Christ as the heavenly, loving, and winsome One. The *ram* speaks of Christ as the consecrated substitute for man.

The GOAT sets forth CHRIST in the likeness of sinful flesh. The goat speaks of Christ as being made sin for us. In the vigor, energy and strength of His manhood, He was hanged on a tree and cursed for you and me; and *thus* cursed because of our sin, He became our goat dying for us, and our scapegoat bearing away our sins into a land of forgetfulness. Christ as our goat and scapegoat blots out our sins as far as the east is from the west.

The slain goat was called the Lord's lot, and thus speaks of atonement, propitiation, redemption, and Calvary.

The living goat was called the people's lot, and speaks of forgiveness, cleansing, and experiential salvation.

This day of atonement affected the whole nation of Israel. It met all the just and righteous claims of God as well as the deepest needs of man. It was the greatest event of the year to the people of God. On this great day of atonement the high priest was compelled to endure numerous inconveniences and humiliations. Separated from home, he must take off his clothes of beauty and put on plain linen garments. It was necessary for Him to fast and pray, and, alone, he must go into the presence of God and make an atonement for all the people. After a very oppressive and exhaustive day he must appear before God, sprinkle the mercy seat with blood, and make an atonement for all the people of God. After such atonement was made the people gathered around him in sympathy and with congratulations. He again put on his garments of glory and beauty, blessed the people, and the people shouted the praises of God.

Aaron was a type of Christ as our Great High Priest. The linen *coat* sets forth his holy *life*. The linen *breeches* speak of his holy *walk*. The linen *girdle* was an emblem of holy *service* while the linen *mitre* on his head sets forth his holy *submission* and subjection to the whole will of God. The *goat* typifies Christ as being made a curse for us.

The dead goat sets forth the death of Christ, while the living goat, going away to a land of forgetfulness, and taking all the sins, failures, mistakes, and shortcomings, of all the people and bearing them away to a land of separation and forgetfulness to be no more remembered against them forever, sets forth experiential salvation.

The linen coat (the spotless life), the breeches (the righteous walk), the girdle (faithful service), and the mitre (constant submission) as well as the blood has a voice for us today. Religion that does not produce holiness of heart and life is a false religion. The decisions of boards, decrees of councils, opinions of men, and past practices and precedents are no account whatever unless they are in harmony with the Word of God. God's word settles everything for the Christian. The Word of God must govern every conscience, and guide every life, for we shall be judged by the standards of the Word of God.

HOLINESS

"It breathes in the prophecy, thunders in the law, murmurs in the narrative, whispers in the promises, supplicates in the prayers, sparkles in the poetry, resounds in the songs, speaks in the types, glows in the imagery, voices in the language, and burns in the spirit of the whole scheme, from the Alpha to the Omega, from its beginning to its end. Holiness! holiness needed, holiness a present duty, a present privilege, a present enjoyment, is the progress and completeness of the Bible's wondrous theme!"—BISHOP FOSTER.

12

HOLINESS

Lev. 19

The standard of God in both the Old and the New Testament is *perfection*. A perfect and holy God could not be satisfied with anything less than perfection or holiness in His people. The grand incentive to holiness of heart is the holiness of God. We worship a holy God. God desires holiness in His children. He is our Father and He calls us to holiness. He not only calls to holiness but He demands and commands us to be holy and His commands are His enablings.

"Ye shall be holy."

Holiness of heart is to be followed by holiness in the life, holiness in the home, holiness in our business, holiness in the meat market, everyday holiness, practical holiness.

I. Holiness in the home.

"Ye shall fear every man his mother and his father." God, the God of the Bible, the God who made you, the God who has redeemed you, the God who cares for you and is intensely interested in you, calls attention to your high privilege, duty and responsibility, God says:

"Son, daughter, hear me!"

"Ye shall fear every man his mother and his father."

"Honour thy father and thy mother."

Do not belittle the mother who gave you birth. Do not grieve her. Do not call your father "the old man" or your mother "the old woman." Never be guilty of calling them *old fogies* and *back numbers*.

II. Holiness in your business.

"Ye shall not steal, neither deal falsely, neither lie one to another."

You cannot go to heaven if you tell lies. You cannot steal or lie and make heaven your home.

It is amazing how some people will lie, cheat and deceive and yet profess religion.

We must be honest with man as well as holy before God if we expect to make heaven our home.

If your house or business is worth only five thousand dollars, do not argue that it is worth ten thousand dollars.

Avoid the slimy, slick serpentlike way of doing business and then think you are shrewd and that the rest of mankind are sissies. Put away all false dealings in the home, church and market place. Be honest and be truthful.

III. Holiness in everyday life.

(1) "Thou shalt not respect the person of the poor."

A poor man comes to church. Very few people pay attention to him. A rich man comes with rings on his tobacco stained fingers and a sparkling lodgepin stuck in his tie. Watch the difference in the reception. The poor and weak ought to be as welcome to your home and church as the rich and powerful.

(2) "Thou shalt not go up and down as a tale-bearer" (verse 16).

This is holiness in practice as well as profession. This is holiness in secret as well as in church. It is impossible to keep the grace of God in your hearts and indulge in gossip, tale-bearings, and unkind criticisms of others. You cannot keep saved and go around tittle-tattling, fault finding, and tale-bearing. If you desire to keep hot religion in your heart you must keep your big mouth shut. Many people have grieved the Spirit by their profitless talk and tale-bearing. Some of you had better make wrongs right before you land in hell. You cannot go to heaven with hell's brimstone in your heart and the whispering, tale-bearing, backbiting devil in your mouth. You had better padlock your non-stop press-news box. Your buzz machine needs a self controller attached or you are headed for the backsliders' ACELDAMA.

HEAR ME! One of the most alarming signs of approach to the dead line is the fact that the Holy Spirit no longer checks some people in connection with their tale-bearing.

"Thou shalt not steal."

"Thou shalt not kill."

"Thou shalt not go up and down as a tale-bearer."

You must line up with this truth or make your bed in hell.

(3) "Thou shalt in any wise rebuke thy neighbour and not suffer sin upon him" (Lev. 19:17).

We are to quietly, lovingly but firmly reprove and rebuke sin whether in low or in high places.

To a person who persists in taking God's name in vain we are to remind of the command, "Thou shalt not take the name of the Lord thy God in vain."

We are not to smile and assent to smutty stories told to us or repeated in our hearing, but sincerely and earnestly reprove and rebuke the teller of such stories. If there were more rebukes there would be much less brazen faced sinning on our streets and in our cities. The church of today is too soft and too dumb. We must speak out against sin both in private and in public.

(4) "Thou shalt not bear any grudge against the children of thy people."

Churlishness among the people of God is unthinkable. Sullenness is sin. Crabbedness in a converted person is equal to crookedness. Fits of sulking, giving black looks, scowling, pouting, going around with a hang dog look are almost unpardonable in a Christian. We ought to give up our crusty, crabbed, surly, sore as a boil, spleenish and perverse ways or give up our profession of salvation. Cross-grained and cantankerous individuals need to have their conversion converted. Refractory and intractable professing Christians need to be pulverized as well as purified.

Scowling, out of sorts, grumpy and glum, splenetic saints need to have their sanctification sanctified.

Maliciousness, spite, dis-kindness, envy, uncharitableness, rancour, venom and churlishness are incompatible with saintship and sanctification.

To plant a thorn in the breast of another believer is devilish and despicable.

Cold blooded, flint hearted grudge-bearers are already half damned. God have mercy on us.

"Thou shalt not bear any grudge."

Hear me you ill-disposed, ill-natured, spiteful, caustic, unamiable, marble hearted professors of religion. You had better get rid of that damnable, fiendish infernal disposition of yours before you die or you will go to hell despite all your profession. I care not to which church you belong. You may be a charter member of the church but if you bear a grudge against any one you are headed in the wrong way and destined to an unhappy ending. You cannot go to heaven with a grudge in your heart.

You cannot possibly make heaven with spleen in your soul and sourness in your spirit.

Let me tell you something which is much more serious than robbing a bank, or murdering a baby, something much worse than telling lies, stealing or cheating in business. It is to have a sour soul, animosity and hatred in your heart, bitterness and bile in your blood, it is to be implacable and revengeful in your nature, and at swords points in your spirit. I warn you.

FLAT NOSED FOLLOWERS
DWARFED DISCIPLES
CROOKT BACKT CHRISTIANS
SCABBED, SCURVY SAINTS
BROKEN HANDED AND
BROKEN FOOTED BELIEVERS

"The mountains and plains, the rivers and seas, the birds and beasts, the flowers and trees, the thunder and lightning, the dew and rain, the sun, moon, and the stars, with the wind, earthquake, and the storm are pressed into service to set forth the power and wisdom and love of God and to inculcate in its human and divine relationships the ever pressing duty of man."

13

FLAT NOSED, CROOK BACKT
SCABBED, DWARFED, BROKEN

(Lev. 21:18-20)

All scripture is given by inspiration of God and is profitable. The first man (Adam), the first martyr (Abel), the first preacher of righteousness (Noah) the first person offered to God as a sacrifice (Isaac), the first leader of God's people (Moses), the first high priest (Aaron), and the first priest-prince (Melchizedek) were all types, prefigurings, or foreshadowings of the one great man, the one righteous prophet, the one leader and high priest, the one true prophet and king, i.e., our Lord Jesus Christ.

Adam, head of a new race, the first man, made in the image of God, formed of the virgin earth, having a body akin to the earth and a spirit akin to God, Lord and ruler of all, with all things delivered into his hands, filled with wisdom and truth, was a foreshadowing of the last Adam and the second man, Christ Jesus. As far as the scripture is concerned there have been only two men in the history of the race—the first man—Adam, and the second man—Jesus Christ. All other men are wrecks because of sin. We have never seen a man as God made him, and we never will see such a man until we see Christ. Adam was a great type of our Lord Jesus Christ. Was Adam formed of the virgin earth? Christ was formed of the virgin Mary! Was Adam in the image and likeness of God, full of wisdom and truth? Christ was the manifestation of God, full of grace and truth. Do all men live because of Adam? Was Adam the Lord and ruler of all? Were all things delivered unto Adam? Christ shall yet be King of kings and Lord of lords. Thus we could proceed dealing with Melchizedek, Moses and Aaron, etc., showing that they all beautifully typify our Lord Jesus Christ.

As Aaron typified Christ, so the sons of Aaron typify believers as the sons of God. The priests were to be sons of the high priest by birth, they were called, they were anointed, and they were to be holy; they were consecrated, to serve in the tabernacle; they carried the ark of the covenant on their shoulders, taught the law, blew the trumpets, and showed forth the praises of God. Their old garments were put off and new garments were put on. They were to be without blemish in heart and life. They were set apart as God's chosen, special, and peculiar people. A blind man or one who was lame, or was broken footed, broken handed, crook backt or dwarfed, or scurvy, scabbed, or unfruitful, or a man who had a flat nose or anything superfluous could not enter into the holy of holies or serve the Lord acceptably as consecrated and ordained ministers.

All believers are priests, and are called to minister to the Lord. Some are especially called to separate themselves from the common pursuits of men and give themselves without distraction to the service of the Lord.

The Old Testament ministers were typical of what New Testament ministers ought to be. Were the priests to be sons? We too must be born again before we can serve God acceptably.

Must the priests belong to the family before they could worship? We must be born anew into the family of God before we can worship aright. Joining church and signing cards will not suffice. We must be born again.

Must the priest be consecrated and holy? We too must receive the unction of the Holy One, and, with hearts purified by the baptism with the Holy Ghost and fire, we shall then be able to render holy service to the Lord.

Did the priests carry the ark across the sandy desert? We too must bear the ark, our Lord Jesus Christ, so that all may see and know Him, whom to know is life eternal.

Was it the duty of the priest to blow the trumpet? It is our duty and responsibility to give the trumpet of testimony no uncertain sound. We must not fail to declare the whole counsel of God. We must not fail to warn men and women to flee from the wrath to come. We also must teach the Word and show forth the praises of Him who hath called us out of darkness into His marvelous light.

Were the priests to part with their old garments and be clothed with new garments? We must say goodby to our past manner of life, and, as new creatures in

Christ Jesus having put off the old man and having put on the new, we must keep ourselves unspotted from the world.

Were the priests to wash their bodies in pure water? We too must keep ourselves clean, and if we walk in the Light the blood cleanseth from all sin.

We must not only realize the necessity of being sanctified wholly as a definite act of God's grace, but we must realize the importance and necessity of keeping clean by walking in all the light shed across our pathway. Turning to the text we find these things specifically mentioned.

1. *The blind.* A blind man requires some other human hand to lead and guide or assist him. He must walk much of the time in uncertainty and trust largely to his sense of touch and sound. Being blind he is unable to see the ordinary objects of everyday life. A blind man could not serve the Lord acceptably. What a host of spiritually blind preachers and people there are around us.

2. *The lame.* A lame man cannot walk straight. He makes crooked paths; his steps are uneven. He is up and down, and down and up. He has life, such as it is, and can walk, but he is very uncertain. In slippery places a misstep will bring disastrous results. The spiritually lame are legion. They are at the altar in almost every camp and revival. They are a serious problem to preacher and God. Unable to walk straight, they are up and down and down and up, constantly making crooked paths.

3. *The flat-nosed.* Any person whose smeller is affected is always in great danger of contracting disease. On the foreign fields a good smeller is an absolute essential to long life and usefulness. We need good smellers to discern when things are wrong. There are some people who fail to see the difference between Bible holiness and popular holiness. Some people will listen to a tobacco smoking, card playing, movie attending preacher, and because he happens to mention holiness or sanctification in his sermon, they put him down as a holiness preacher. Their smeller is not working good. A certain preacher bought a fifty cent chance on an automobile and could neither see nor smell anything wrong. Others link up with godless secret societies and lodges and declare that they neither see nor smell anything harmful.

They are in dire need of the great Physician to fix up their eyesight and their smeller. They need their flat nose straightened and fixed. They ought to seek the divine face lifter. Other people and preachers go to fairs, shows, festivals, bazaars, movies, and even dances, and they can neither see nor smell the dangers to their spiritual life and well being. They are blind and flat nosed, and cannot serve God acceptably.

4. *Broken footed.* A person with a broken foot is unable to walk unless he uses helps such as crutches. He must have some visible means of support or he cannot even walk to church or prayermeeting. Visiting the sick or the widows and fatherless are each and all out of the question. He finds it impossible to run with pa-

tience the race which is set before him. Walking circumspectly or walking as He walked is impossible. He needs the great Physician before he can serve the Lord and walk before Him with a perfect heart.

5. *The broken handed.* A man with a broken hand cannot work any more than a man with a broken foot can walk. These broken handed and broken footed people may be good bench warmers and loud talkers and great professors, but when it comes to lifting loads, carrying burdens, and pulling and pushing they are conspicuous by their absence. They do not even bother themselves to give a cup of cold water (never mind a cup of hot coffee) in the name of a disciple. They never entertain any angels unawares for they never entertain any one at all. They are broken handed. Men may be bleeding and dying on every street, but they never bind their wounds or pour in oil or wine. They have barely life enough to draw their own breath. They are in great need of the great Physician. Preaching, teaching, and singing do not help them. Their broken hands and broken feet need fixing and straightening. A dairy of unseparated milk, a carload of the grapes of Eshcol, and a barrel of honey would not effect a cure. They need the ruthless bone-setter. It is not nursing or plasters that are needed but the bone-setter. They need, and must have, the great Physician or they will be unable to serve either God or man.

It is with great pain that a broken handed person either pays tithes or gives an offering.

6. *Crook backt*. Something has gone wrong with the spine. The tendency is to droop and stoop. The eyes are on the earth most of the time. It is very difficult for them to look up. They are crook backt. Balaam was a crook backt preacher; Achan was one of the crook backt children of Israel; Judas was a crook backt apostle; Esau and Simon, together with Ananias and Sapphira, were all typical crook backt professors. Nothing, and no one, short of the great Physician, can straighten up and straighten out the spine and enable us to walk uprightly and to set our affections on the things above.

7. *A dwarf*. A dwarf is a person whose growth has stopped short of God's standard. A seventy year old baby is an unseemly sight. It must be nursed and dangled on the knee and entertained, is easily offended, quickly goes up the miff tree, and constantly requires some one to stroke the fur the right way. The Church is full of spiritual pigmies and spiritual runts. It is full of people whose spiritual growth has been arrested. They are seen in a meeting house on Sunday morning if it does not rain or snow. They put a nickel or a quarter in the offering basket and wonder why the preacher is always taking up offerings. Something has stopped their growth.

8. *Scurvy and scabbed*. Scabs and scurvy on the outside are evidences of something wrong on the inside. The inside has been wrong for quite a while and now it is showing itself on the outside. It is apparent to all that something is wrong on the inside. A pianist went up

the miff tree because the song leader asked her to speed up a little in her playing. The scurvy appeared at once, and it became apparent to all that something was wrong. A sister became peeved because she was not asked to sing a special at the revival, and the scab was apparent to all. There are a host of scurvy and scabbed people who cannot enjoy the holy of holies or the continued presence of the God of the Bible. We need the great Physician to cure our spiritual blindness by the magic two-fold touch of His omnipotent power. He alone can cure our lameness, fix up our smeller, straighten out our crooked spines, and make us complete so that we may worship the Lord in the beauty of holiness, and serve Him acceptably with reverence and with godly fear.

THE SEVEN FEASTS

"Get right with God," say the offerings.
"Keep right with God," say the feasts.

14

THE FEASTS OF THE LORD

Lev. 23

In the early history of God's people as found in the Old Testament, there were special seasons of fellowship and feasting called, holy convocations. These holy convocations or feasts of the Lord were something similar to our holiness campmeetings.

The first of these regular holiness campmeetings was called *the feast of the Sabbath*. The first Sabbath mentioned in the Bible is in Genesis 2. God, having ended His work which He had made, rested on the seventh day, and God blessed the seventh day and sanctified it because in it He had rested from all His work which He had created and made. In Exodus twenty, Israel was commanded to remember the Sabbath day, to keep it holy. This weekly Sabbath of rest was to become a regular feast of the Lord. Jesus came into the world to bring peace and rest, and there can be no rest either in time or in eternity outside of Jesus Christ. The second of these holiness campmeetings was called *the feast of the passover*. Israel was commanded at even on the fourteenth day of the month to celebrate the Lord's passover. The feast of the passover was held to commemorate their deliverance from Egypt. Egypt is a type of this present evil world; Pharaoh is a type of the devil; the lamb was a type of Christ; and the salvation of God's people from Pharaoh and Egypt foreshadowed our salvation through our Lord Jesus Christ. The passover lamb died on the fourteenth day of April, the feast of the passover was held on the fourteenth day of April, and Christ died on the fourteenth day of April.

The passover lamb died in Egypt at *even* and the passover feast was to be celebrated at *even;* Christ, our passover, sacrificed for us, died at *even*. It was between the two evenings that the lamb died in Egypt, that the passover feast was celebrated in Canaan, and that Christ died on Calvary.

The third holy convocation was *the feast of unleavened bread*. Bread speaks of fellowship, communion, and feasting. Leaven is a type of evil; hence the feast of unleavened bread speaks of separation from evil.

The next feast of the Lord was *the feast of first fruits*. When Israel reaped the harvest of the fields they were commanded to bring a sheaf of the first fruits and wave the sheaf before the Lord. This was to be done on the morrow after the Sabbath, and they were forbidden to eat either bread or parched corn until they had brought an offering unto the Lord. The morrow after the Sabbath was the first day of the week, and thus was held on Sunday.

The sheaf of ripened grain which was waved before the Lord sets forth the resurrection of Christ. Thus the resurrection of Christ on a Sunday morning was strikingly typified by this feast of first fruits.

The Jewish Sabbath was held on our Saturday; the morrow after the Sabbath was thus our Sunday or the Lord's day. How marvelous is the Word of God. Every year of their obedient history the children of Israel were celebrating the resurrection of Christ which took place on the first Easter Sunday morning. Selah!

Since they were forbidden to eat anything until they had brought an offering unto the Lord, they were setting forth the important truth that God must be first in our hearts and in our lives.

The next holiness convention held by the children of Israel was *the feast of weeks*. Fifty days after the wave offering of first fruits Israel was to bring two wave loaves of two tenth deals of fine flour baked with leaven, seven lambs without blemish, one young bullock, two rams, and one kid of the goats, to the priest who was to wave an offering before the Lord.

This feast also was to be held on the morrow after the Sabbath. The two loaves of two tenth deals of fine flour typify our Lord Jesus Christ as the bread of life to both *Jews and Gentiles*. Flour is obtained through a grain of wheat dying, and then coming up in resurrection, life, and power. Christ was that grain or corn of wheat. He died and rose again and has become the Bread of Life.

Fine flour is obtained through crushing, pounding, and beating; this crushing, pounding, and grinding sets forth the sufferings of Christ.

The two loaves were typical of both Jews and Gentiles. The presence of leaven in the two loaves sets forth the fact of carnality in the hearts of God's people. The fifty days after the wave offering of first fruits strikingly foreshadows the day of Pentecost when the disciples with leaven in their hearts met together in the upper room.

The seven lambs typified the perfect Lamb of God while the one young bullock sets forth Christ as the true servant of God and man. The two rams set forth Christ as the consecrated substitute for both Jews and Gentiles while the kid of the goats speaks of Christ made sin for us.

The feast of the passover thus typifies the death of Christ.

The feast of the first fruits typifies the resurrection of Christ.

The feast of weeks typified the day of Pentecost.

We are now living in the Pentecostal dispensation and it is very striking to notice that right in the middle of the chapter setting forth these feasts we have this remarkable scripture:

"When ye reap the harvest of your land thou shalt not make clean riddance of the corners of thy field when thou reapest, neither shalt thou gather any gleaning of thy harvest, thou shalt leave them unto the poor and the *stranger*."

Provision was thus made for the Gentiles, the Old Testament "whosoever will." This scripture sets forth the evangelization of the world in this pentecostal dispensation.

When God called Abram and started him out on his way to Canaan, God gave him a promise that in him all the families of the earth would be blessed. Down through the centuries God has had the *"whosoever will"* upon His heart and in His plans. When the covenant was renewed to Isaac and again to Jacob the promise also was renewed that through them all the families of the earth would be blessed.

When Israel left Egypt the *"whosoever"* who would take a lamb and sprinkle the blood would be protected from the wrath of the destroying angel.

In the tabernacle and later in the temple provision was made for the *"whosoever will"* among the Gentiles.

Joseph was to be a fruitful bough by a well and his branches were to run over the wall to the *"whosoever will."*

God gave to Abraham the promise of a DUST seed which is Israel. On another occasion God gave to Abraham the promise of a STAR seed which is spiritual Israel or the Church of Christ. The third time that the promise was repeated the STAR seed was put first. Thus in Genesis the first was last and the last was first. The children of Israel were warned that God could graft the wild olive tree into the trunk; thus the Gentile *whosoever* was remembered.

Job was neither a Hebrew nor an Israelite nor a Jew, but he was saved and sanctified and successful.

Ruth and Rahab were both sinners of the Gentiles, but were included in the glorious whosoever will of God's grace.

Melchizedek, the most puzzling of all Old Testament characters, was neither a Hebrew nor a Jew, but he, nevertheless, administered the sacramental bread and wine to Abraham. Thus, two thousand years before Christ was born the emblems of His broken body and shed blood were given to Abraham. Naaman was healed from his leprosy and was amongst the Gentile whosoevers.

The Syro-phœnician woman was given a whole loaf of bread because she was willing to take the place of a Gentile dog.

The Roman centurion's servant was healed, for Jesus was the son of MAN as well as the son of God. Christ is not only the Light for the children of Israel, but He is also the Light of the World.

At His birth He was visited by the Wise Men of the East. The wise men of the West also sought Him saying, "Sir, we would see Jesus."

It was a colored man from Africa who helped him to bear His cross. That cross was for the whosoever will.

Peter was given a special vision in order to show him that the unclean and unworthy whosoevers were included in redemption's plans.

The commission given to Paul the Apostle was to preach the gospel to the Gentiles. God so loved the world from Genesis through to Malachi, as well as in

John 3:16, that He gave His only begotten Son that whosoever believeth in Him should not perish but have everlasting life.

The seven feasts of the Lord as recorded in Lev. 23 include the poor and the stranger and thus the whosoever will was remembered even in the Levitical economy.

The gleanings of the harvest were to be left for the whosoever will.

Israel was solemnly warned that if they should prove unfaithful the vineyard would be given to the whosoever will. Down through the ages God has planned and provided for the whosoever will.

Thus between the feast of Weeks (Pentecost) and the feast of Trumpets (second Advent) Israel was commanded to leave the *gleanings* for the *whosoever will*. How marvellous are the ways of God.

The next feast was *the feast of trumpets*. The silver trumpet sounded, and all Israel gathered themselves together for the soul stirring feast of trumpets.

This feast of trumpets strikingly foreshadows the second coming of Christ. When He comes again the sleeping saints will be resurrected, the living saints will be raptured, and the children of Israel will again be gathered to their own land.

The passover feast speaks of the death of Christ on the fourteenth day of April.

The wave offering feast sets forth the resurrection of Christ on Sunday morning April the seventeenth.

The feast of weeks typified the day of Pentecost fifty days after the resurrection of Christ.

The gleaning for the poor and the stranger in the corners of the field foreshadowed present day evangelism and missions to the Gentiles. "Go" and "Lo."

The feast of trumpets sets forth the second coming of Christ together with:

1. The resurrection of the sleeping saints,

2. The rapture of the living saints,

3. The regathering of Israel unto her own land. Selah!

The next holy convocation or feast of the Lord was *the feast of tabernacles*. Israel was to take the boughs of goodly trees, branches of palm trees, the boughs of thick trees, and willows of the brook, and rejoice before the Lord seven days. Seven days in every year were thus to be spent dwelling in booths. This feast, which continued for seven days, was called the feast of tabernacles. The feast of tabernacles typifies the millennium.

Israel shall once again dwell in booths with every man under his own vine and under his own fig tree.

It is deeply instructive to notice that these holiness campmeetings were called Feasts of the Lord and NOT feasts of Israel.

When Israel was celebrating the feast of the passover, God was looking forward to another passover. God was feasting on the sacrifice of Christ on the cross of Calvary.

When Israel was celebrating the feast of first fruits,

God was looking forward to the first Easter Sunday morning, and He feasted on a resurrected Christ.

When Israel was celebrating the Feast of Weeks, God's heart was upon a few of His children in an upper room in Jerusalem, who, when the day of pentecost was fully come, were all filled with the Holy Ghost. God was feasting in anticipation of the great and glad day when experiential holiness of heart could be bestowed upon the waiting apostles. Hence these feasts were not feasts of Israel but feasts of the Lord.

When Israel was celebrating the feast of trumpets, God was anticipating the home coming of His redeemed saints.

The feast of the passover pointed on to Calvary, the feast of first fruits pointed to the resurrection of Christ, the feast of weeks pointed forward to the day of Pentecost, the feast of trumpets pointed on to the resurrection and rapture of the saints and the regathering of Israel while the feast of tabernacles foreshadowed the coming of the glad millennial day.

The next great feast was *the Feast of Jubilee*.

In the history of the children of Israel every fiftieth year was celebrated as a jubilee year. In the year of jubilee all bonds were broken, all prisoners were set free, all possessions automatically reverted to their original owners, all exiles were brought home, all absent and living loved ones returned home, and all things were restored.

The year of jubilee was a foreshadowing of the new heavens and the new earth, when all things shall be restored, and Paradise, lost by sin, will be restored by Christ. The feast of passover and first fruits and weeks and trumpets and tabernacles and jubilee set forth the whole history of redemption. These holy convocations prefigure the whole course of time.

The arrangement is so wonderful, so marvelous, and so divine that we are constrained to bow our heads, consecrate our lives, submit our hearts and our minds, and place our present, our future, and our all, at the disposal of the supernatural inspirer of the Book of books, which we call the Bible. Here in one brief chapter of forty-four verses we have the whole history of redemption, and the setting forth of the whole course of time.

THE PURE CANDLESTICK

"Let me reiterate my conviction that no one knows enough to show that the true text of the Old Testament in its true interpretation is not true. The evidence in our possession has convinced me that at "sundry times and in divers manners God spake in time past unto the fathers by the prophets," that the Old Testament in Hebrew "being immediately inspired by God" has "by his singular care and providence been kept pure in all ages"; and that, when the wisdom of men and the law of God had alike failed to save humanity, in the fullness of time, when all the preparation was complete, God sent forth His Son to confound the wisdom of man and to redeem those who come under the law. Thank God for the Holy Oracles. Thank Him yet more for "the unspeakable gift" of His love, who brought life and immortality to light in His gospel."—DR. ROBERT DICK WILSON (A Scientific Investigation of the Old Testament, p. 12).

15

THE PURE CANDLESTICK

(Lev. 24:1-4)

"And the Lord spake unto Moses, saying, Command the children of Israel, that they bring unto thee pure oil olive beaten for the light, to cause the lamps to burn continually. Without the vail of the testimony, in the tabernacle of the congregation, shall Aaron order it from the evening unto the morning before the Lord continually: it shall be a statute for ever in your generations. He shall order the lamps upon the pure candlestick before the Lord continually" (Lev. 24:1-4).

1. Made of Pure Gold.

The main shaft typifies Christ. The seven branches typify believers. The branches were beaten out of one solid piece of gold. "I am the vine, ye are the branches" (John 15).

The process of beating, beautifully typifies the sufferings of Christ as the God-man in order to be the light of the world. The beating was done outside of the Holy of Holies; thus Christ must needs come out from the presence of God to suffer and die.

The candlestick or lampstand was the only light in

the holy place. Christ is not only the light, but He is the *only* light of the world.

The branches were beaten *out of the side* of the candlestick. Believers, like Eve, have been taken out of the side of the second Adam.

The strength of the Branches was in the shaft, for without Christ believers are helpless.

2. Made in order to give light and shine.

They were made *not* for entertainment or show, but for light in the darkness.

It was to shine before the Lord and not for the approval of men.

It was to shine upon the table of fellowship and communion, for where two or three are gathered together in Christ's name THERE He is in the midst.

3. Filled and kept filled with oil.

The oil typifies the Holy Spirit, who filled Christ and filled the apostles. Pentecost was the pouring in of the oil into the waiting expectant apostles. They were all filled with the Holy Ghost. Not only were they filled on the Day of Pentecost, but they were kept filled as they kept in the path of obedience and faith.

Tongs and snuffers were provided for trimming, for the lamps needed trimming in order to keep them clean. There is no mention of an EXTINGUISHER. God's people may sometimes need TRIMMING in order that the light may shine farther and brighter.

4. Was to burn continually.

The Holy Spirit is exhaustless. The believer is to be kept by the power of God through faith. The fires of holy love and zeal are to be kept burning brightly on the altar of the believer's heart.

THE HOLY PERFUME
CHRIST

"In vain do we look through the entire biography of Jesus for a single stain or the slightest shadow on His moral character. There never lived a more harmless being on earth. He injured nobody, He took advantage of nobody. He never spoke an improper word, He never committed a wrong action. He exhibited a uniform elevation above the objects, opinions, pleasures, and passions of this world, and disregard to riches, displays, fame, and favor of men. 'No vice that has a name can be thought of in connection with Jesus Christ. Ingenious malignity looks in vain for the faintest trace of self-seeking in His motives; sensuality shrinks abashed from His celestial purity; falsehood can leave no stain on Him who is incarnate truth; injustice is forgotten beside His errorless equity; the very possibility of avarice is swallowed up in His benignity and love; the very idea of ambition is lost in His divine wisdom and divine self-abnegation.' "—Dr. Schaff.

16

THE HOLY PERFUME

Questions of Life

Life is one floodtide of Question Marks.

Why? How? What? When? Whence? Whither? Where?

1. Why are we here?

Not by accident.

Not by chance.

We are a part of God's gigantic plan.

He has a blue print for each life.

We are here to glorify God.

2. From whence came evil?

In the beginning God. Here is the beginning of good.

Lucifer rebelled against God in *eternity* and became Satan as Adam rebelled against God in *time* and became a sinner. Here is the beginning of EVIL.

3. Why are the best things in life seemingly so obscure and intangible?

"The things which are seen are temporal." God is a Spirit and spiritual things are spiritually discerned, therefore, ye must be born again, born anew, born from above. The spiritual world is just as real as the physical world but it takes *faith* to make it real and faith is impossible without repentance and man will not repent because he loves darkness and sin rather than light and holiness.

4. Why is it so much easier to sin than not to sin?

God created man upright. Man sinned and was separated from God. Separated from God it becomes easy to sin.

Christ became a Jacob's ladder and bridged the gulf. Man may get back to God. *In the center of God's will* it is easier to do right than it is to do wrong. Therefore it is not easier to sin than not to sin if you do not want to sin. It is much easier for me to do right than it would be for me to do wrong. I have no desire to do wrong. Thank God.

5. Why is the heart of man so constituted that it can never be satisfied?

The heart of man which has been vacated by God because of disobedience is a bottomless pit in itself. It can not be satisfied without God and holiness. The heart was intended to be God's temple. The heart was made to be filled with God, and neither money—houses, lands— nor anything else can satisfy the heart of man.

6. Why do the wicked prosper?

Reformers of all ages have fought an uphill battle. It is next to impossible to be right and popular at the same time.

Satan is at present the god of this present evil world in which we live. He offered the kingdoms of the world and the glory of them (never once mentioning the sorrows) to Christ if Christ would only worship him. That which Christ rejected has been accepted by others and hence the wicked for the time prosper, but wait a while for "What shall it profit, . . . if he shall gain the whole world and lose his own soul."

7. Why should Christ suffer?

This question is answered in the book of Leviticus and emphasized in this chapter now before us.

Moses was commanded to take sweet spices—stacte, onycha, and galbanum all evenly mixed with pure frankincense and make *a pure and holy perfume*. These different ingredients were to be beaten very small, and then placed on a brazen altar in the holiest of all.

All this speaks of Christ. Christ is not only our Lamb slain, our Shepherd and Guide, our Ark, our Ram, our Pillar of Fire, our Tree cut down, our Bread and Water of Life, our Substitute, our Captain, our Great High Priest, our Bullock, our Goat, our Dove, our Offering, our Rock, our Savior, and our coming King, But He is our all in all. He is our Holy Perfume.

The pounding and beating of these special spices into very small pieces foreshadow the intense sufferings of Christ. Through His offering, His sufferings, His sacrifice, and His intercession we have access unto the Father. We present the holy perfume of the spotless, sacrificial, sweet, HOLY, pure life of Christ and we are accepted in the Beloved. No imitations or comparisons were to be made, for Christ cannot be imitated and Christ cannot be compared. Buddha, Confucius, Russell, Eddy, Smith, White, Krishnamura and Mohammed are all in a different class. There can be no comparisons. The study of comparative religions does not include Christianity.

Christianity stands by itself. Buddha's perfume, like Russell's prayers and Mohammed's curses, get no farther than the nose of man.

No life or prayer or work can ever rise into the nostrils of God without Christ being All and in all.

God cannot accept anything nor any one outside of Christ. The race is doomed, whether infants or adults, rich or poor, saint or sinner, wise or ignorant, English or Hottentot, outside of Christ.

WHAT THEN SHALL I DO WITH JESUS

"In the cross I see the sorrow of God, and in the cross I see the joy of God, for 'it pleased the Lord to bruise him.' In the cross I see the love of God working out through passion and power for the redemption of man. In the cross I see the light of God refusing to make any terms with iniquity and sin and evil. The cross is the historic revelation of the abiding facts within the heart of God."

17

THE ARK OF THE COVENANT
CHRIST

The ark of the covenant was a beautiful foreshadowing of our Lord Jesus Christ. It was the first piece of furniture made for the tabernacle in the wilderness. It was always present and always sufficient. When rightly approached it meant blessing and prosperity. It was made of wood and overlaid with gold. It was anointed with special oil, and sanctified to a special use. Aaron's rod that budded, the law or Ten Commandments, and a pot of manna were placed within the ark, and the lid of the ark, called the mercy seat, covered its sacred contents. It was the meeting place between God and man. It, resting in the holy of holies, was the sign and symbol of the presence of God.

When the children of Israel journeyed, the ark, covered by a blue, scarlet and purple curtain, was carried upon the shoulders of the consecrated and sanctified ministers. It went before the people of God to guide them across a trackless desert. It searched out a place of rest for them. It was always in the midst of the people whenever and wherever they camped. It passed through the river of Jordan before the children of Israel. It brought victory at Jericho and blessing and prosperity to the home of Obed-edom. Despised and rejected by some, it was, nevertheless, accepted and welcomed by others. It brought blasting or blessing according as it was rejected or accepted. When David came to the throne he placed it under a tent, and later Solomon placed it in the temple where it rested on the golden floor of Solomon's temple. The staves were drawn out and its wanderings ended forever.

The ark was the glory of Israel, and, like a clock without a main spring, and a flock of sheep without a shepherd, and a system without a sun, and an arch without a keystone, so was Israel without the ark of the covenant.

It spelled out in letters of fire the certain doom of all false religions and destruction to all who handled it profanely. It was the constant joy and delight of all God's people; even the great King David danced before it with all his might. Without the Ark Israel was always defeated in battle. The relationships of men and women towards the ark determined their cursing and their blessing. Dagon could not stand before it, and Uzzah was smitten while Obed-edom was blessed. It is just the same today. What shall we do *with* the Ark?

What shall we do *to* the Ark? 1 Sam. 5:8 and 6:2.

The ark of the covenant was thus a striking type of Christ.

1. He is the first great essential in order to worship God aright. Church joining is not enough. Card signing will not suffice. Shaking hands with a preacher will not regenerate the soul. Nothing less than a personal accept-

ance of and acquaintance with Jesus Christ will satisfy the heart of either God or man.

2. He is always present with His people and He is always sufficient. He will never leave us nor forsake us. In every emergency and under all circumstances He will prove Himself an all sufficient Savior.

3. The wood speaks of a human Christ while the gold speaks of a divine Christ. He was truly man and truly God.

4. As the ark of the covenant was anointed, so Christ, the true ark, was anointed, consecrated, and sanctified.

5. Aaron's rod that budded sets forth the fact of His resurrection; the manna speaks of Him as the Bread of Life for His people while they are passing through the wilderness on their way to the Canaan of perfect love; and the law inside the ark sets forth the fact that Christ kept for us the perfect law of God.

6. Christ is the meeting place between God and man just as the ark was the meeting place between God and Israel. As the ark was the only meeting place between God and man so it is with Christ. Without Christ men are godless. Whether Methodists or Unitarians, TO BE WITHOUT CHRIST IS TO BE WITHOUT GOD. Men may talk glibly about God, and sing piously such songs as "Nearer My God to Thee," but if they are without Christ they are without God and without hope. "He that honoreth not the Son, honoreth not the Father." Pious platitudes and pompous professionalism will not save. God is NOT with us if we are without Christ.

7. Christ is now in the presence of God for us. The ark rested in the holy of holies. The vail has been rent, and the blood has been sprinkled on the mercy seat, and He ever liveth to make intercession for us. The Holy Spirit intercedes IN us and the Christ on high intercedes FOR us.

8. Christ is to be borne aloft and made known to others. As the little maid carried aloft the name of God to the Gentile Naaman, so we are to make known the name of Christ to the world. Christ will go before us across this trackless, thirsty, desert world. He will seek out a place of rest and will be with us to comfort, protect, and cheer. He is our ever-present cheer-leader.